MW01228609

AND YOU SHALL DECREE A THING

Topical Biblical Declarations That Will
Transform Your Life

Kimberly Jones

Copyright ©2017 Kimberly Jones

All rights reserved. No part of this publication may be reproduced,
stored in a retrieval system, or transmitted in any form or by any
means, electronic, mechanical, recording or otherwise, without the
prior written permission of the author. All quoted scriptures are
taken from King James Version Bible or The Amplified Version
Bible.

Printed in the United States of America

THIS BOOK IS NOT INTENDED TO BE A HISTORY TEXT.
While every effort has been made to check the accuracy of dates,
locations, and historical information, no claims are made as to the
accuracy of such information.

For book orders, author appearance inquiries and interviews, contact
author by email at Livenow@kimberlyj.net All rights reserved.

ISBN: 1519153066
ISBN-13: 978-1519153067

DEDICATION

I dedicate this book to my family- my awesome husband, Louis, my lovely children, Kayla and Justin; and my grandson, Kingston, all of whom have been my greatest inspiration as a wife, mother, grandmother and now…….. author.

ACKNOWLEDGMENTS

I give thanks to my Heavenly Father who enabled me, by the inspiration of the Holy Spirit, to create this collection of declarations based upon His infallible, unfaltering, empowering Word.

CONTENTS

FOREWARD

Hebrew 4:12 states "For the word of God is alive and active. Sharper than any double-edged sword, it penetrates even to dividing soul and spirit, joints and marrow; it judges the thoughts and attitudes of the heart." (NIV)

From this scripture, we see that God's word is not passive, but very active in nature. The wording supports this fact with the use of descriptors such as "sharper," "penetrates," "dividing," and "judging." It is apparent, based upon this language, that the word of God has power. However, if it is not activated its power goes untapped, and there is no penetrating, dividing or judging. That's a problem.

However, there is no need to fret. *And You Shall Decree A Thing* is the answer to that problem. In this book, Kimberly Jones uses the power of decreeing and declaring to activate God's word in the lives of those who will pick it up and follow its instructions.

I am a witness to the effectiveness of using declarations as a weapon of warfare against the enemy. In Kimberly's previous work, 40-Days of Biblical Declarations, the efficiency of this practice was established and verified by the masses of people who took on the challenge of opening up their mouths and releasing God's word through faith. I am in that number of those who have joined the movement of decreeing and declaring and watching God move. The testimonies are endless of those who have introduced this spiritual discipline into their lives.

Kimberly started this journey of decreeing and declaring a few years ago and has not stopped since day one. She has touched the lives of so many people all across the world by initiating this movement of "faith by works" in her church, through her business pursuits, and in ministry. She has even gone as far as to create a platform for sharing these God-inspired declarations on social media platforms such as Facebook and Periscope. It's as if there is no end to her passion and purpose of getting God's word to the four corners of the earth.

I am convinced that the practice of decreeing and declaring is in Kimberly's blood and it is truly an intrinsic part of who she is. As her husband, I have seen her work tirelessly at getting the word of God out into the world through her books and other ministry efforts. As I have watched her push through adversity and just plain moments of burnout, I am convinced that this is a God-ordained assignment for her.

This is her second declaration-focused book, and I am sure it will not be her last. Although there are many topics covered in this book, I am convinced that there are many more waiting to be birthed out of this woman of the Word. I don't know what your life is presently in need of. But, what I do know is this; if you passionately apply the declarations shared in this book, you will see your life forever transformed.

If you only believe and do not doubt in your heart, you will experience the transformational power of decreeing and declaring. This book is a keeper; it's content will never be outdated or irrelevant. I thank God for giving my wife the inspiration to write this book, which I know will be a blessing to many.

Apostle Louis D. Jones, Jr.
Senior Pastor, Prevailing Love Worship Center

INTRODUCTION

The Creative Power of Words

In the beginning, God created the heaven and the earth. And the earth was without form, and void; and darkness was upon the face of the deep. And the spirit of God moved upon the face of the waters. And God said, Let there be light and there was light.
Genesis 1:1-3(KJV)

It doesn't matter how many times I read the book of Genesis; I am always amazed at the story of creation that is outlined within its pages. When I think about how God, in all of His majesty, created something out of nothing, it reminds me of just how powerful He really is. Just think about, the Bible states that the earth was without form, void, and there was nothing but darkness. The Spirit of God was hovering over this mass collection of nothingness, and then all of a sudden something shifted. A voice began to speak into this formless, void, and dark existence and the birth of creation was set into motion. That voice, of course, belonged to God and it produced God-sized results. The rest of the first chapter of Genesis details the creative process of God that changed nothing into something. Everything was created over the course of the next six days from light, to the heavens and earth, to crawling, flying, and swimming

3

beasts........culminating with God's greatest creation.....man.

The one thing that intrigues me most is how simple the process seems to have been. From what I read in the Bible, it did not seem to be a very laborious process for God. As a matter of fact, it appears to have been quite contrary to that. There is no indication that there was a lot of disruption as God exercised the creative power of His words to create what we know today to be the universe.

We don't read of lightening striking, or thunder clamoring as God separated the heavens and the earth, and dry land from the seas. We don't read about any explosions that occur as the night is separated from the day. There is no indication that the earth trembled when the earth gave way and began producing grass, the herb yielding seed and fruit bearing trees. It was a simple process of "call and response."

"In Genesis 1:3, the word of God states this..."And God said, Let there be light, and there was light." That's it. And every other part of creation that ensued was exactly the same. God said......and there was. Call and response. God called out and commanded what He wanted to appear, and there was a response from out of the darkness. The call was so powerful that every place that was void, without form, and dark had no choice but to relent to the authority of God's command and come to life.

This whole idea of "call and response," upon which the universe was built, has great implication for us, as the children of God. Just like everything else in the universe, we were also created by God. However, there was more involved in the human aspect of creation. Genesis 1:26 states, "And God said, Let us create man in our image, after our likeness…..". In Genesis 2:7 we see that God actually formed man out of the dust of the ground and breathed the breath of life into his nostrils and man became a living soul. We see that God took a more personal approach in creating man. No other part of creation took on the image and likeness of God. No other part of creation was delegated dominion authority. No other part of creation was formed by the hands of God and brought to life by the breath of God. Only man.

This is where the connection between the creation of the universe, creation of man and biblical declarations unfolds. At some time or another, we all experience what I call "The Dark Ages." Meaning, that at times our lives will seem ….without form….void……and dark, just like the universe was before God's words came forth. During our "Dark Ages" seasons it feels as if we have no power to produce anything in any area of our lives. Everything is silent and still. This time of "darkness" is not the same for everyone. Others may find themselves in a season where their life lacks order and progress in some capacity or another. Just when you get one area of your life running pretty smoothly, another area becomes unsettled and chaotic.

You know what I mean. Your marriage appears to be progressing in a positive direction, and all of a sudden the children are out of control. The business seems to be thriving, and then out of nowhere, you become sick in your body. How about this one? You are moving along living your life on purpose, and then you find yourself stuck in a season that seems to have no end. Nothing is moving, growing or progressing. What do we do when we find ourselves in these types of situations? We revert to the creation story and pattern ourselves accordingly.

When God was faced with something that was without form, dark, and void, He activated the power of His presence and His words. Remember, Genesis stated that the Spirit was moving over the face of the waters.......and then God spoke. Because we are fashioned in the image, and after the likeness of God, we too should utilize this same strategy when dealing with situations in our lives where we are stuck in darkness or unable to move forward. As God's handiwork, we can look at our situations, activate the presence of God and speak what it is that we need to materialize. This book empowers you to do just that.

God took the time to create us JUST LIKE HIM. He then gave us dominion authority over all the works of His hands. Psalm 8:6 states, "Thou madest him to rule over the works of Your hands. You have put all things under his feet." This scripture is referring to us, the ones that were formed and fashioned in the image and after the likeness of God.

Creating us in His image meant that God made us a representative figure of Himself. We were made to resemble Him. That is awesome when you think about it. God's desire was and still is that we look like Him. If not, He could have just spoken us into existence like He did the rest of creation. But from the very beginning, we were slated to be His likeness in the earth realm.

Personally, I consider that a huge honor, when I think about who God is. When I think about it, this position carries with it great responsibility. God didn't just create us like Him because it was a good idea. He created us like Him so that we could operate like Him. We were given dominion over all the works of His hands from the very beginning of time. We have the authority, just like God, to speak things into existence. There is not one area of our life that should not be impacted by our level of authority. If God was able to speak to darkness and create light, so should we. It is time for us to speak to every area of our lives and by faith, demand a response.

The enemy has been on our track since the beginning of creation. He seduced Eve, and ultimately Adam into handing over their position in the Garden by offering them the forbidden fruit. I believe that if they had thought about their position of authority properly, they could have commanded the devil to leave. Seeing that they had been given dominion over everything that was created, I believe that they had the power to command the serpent and he would've obeyed!

Genesis 1:26 clearly states that man was given dominion over every creeping thing that creepeth upon the earth. If I am not mistaken, Satan falls in this category. The problem was that he understood man's greatness and power more than man himself. That is why the devil works so hard to continue to deceive man into settling for the proverbial apple. The "apple" is anything in your life that has caused you to compromise, and settle as it pertains to fulfilling God's will. Instead of rebuking the devil, Adam and Eve entered into agreement with him by eating the fruit. It's time out for us allowing the enemy to talk us out of the honor of our dominion authority. It is time for us to begin to speak to every area of our lives and command that it line up. We must come out of agreement with the enemy and into agreement with God's word.

In this book, I have identified some relevant areas of our lives that can benefit from diligently decreeing and declaring. It is time out for fighting spiritual battles in the natural realm. Ephesians 6:12 tells us that "We do not wrestle against flesh and blood, but against principalities, powers, rulers of darkness in this world, and spiritual wickedness in high places." It goes on to say that we must put on the whole armor of God.

One of the most important pieces of our armor is the sword of the spirit, which is the Word of God. Why do so many of us go into battle and leave our sword at home? When we decree and declare the Word of God, we should have the expectation of seeing it established in our lives. Again, the reason that we can do this is that we have been given delegated authority in the earth realm to operate in the power of God.

We don't have to sit idly by and allow the enemy to wreak havoc in our lives. It is time for the people of God to stand up in our authority and reclaim our victory. Just like God, we can look at the empty, dark places of our lives and command that light manifest.

One of the essential components necessary for that to occur is unshakable faith. When God spoke to creation and called it forth, there was no doubt in His mind that what He called to be would manifest. He knew what He wanted to create. He had a strategy and a plan for what He wanted to come forth and in what timing and order. You too must know what you are working to develop in your life as you address each area of concern discussed in this book.

This book is going to provide you with Biblical declarations that speak to specific areas of your life. You do not have to start from the beginning of the book and work your way through. Investigate your life, and determine where the darkness is existing. Be strategic about your launch against the devices of the enemy. You may need to begin decreeing and declaring over a marriage that is on the brink of destruction. Or you may want to begin making bold declarations over your finances. It doesn't matter, just take a real close look at your life and determine what needs to be transformed.

Allow the presence of the Lord to invade your atmosphere. Just like the Spirit of God moved upon the face of the waters before God began commanding, welcome the presence of God's spirit to move upon your situations and then begin to speak. Welcome the presence of Holy Spirit into your home, marriage, business, or ministry. The presence of the Holy Spirit is an indication of the power, provision, and protection of God.

Once you acknowledge the need for God to infiltrate every aspect of your life, you can begin to boldly stand in your authority. Check yourself and see if there is anything in you that would prevent such a move from happening in your life. You cannot command things to begin to shift in your life if the presence of God is not in your midst. Allow your faith to be stirred as you begin to decree the word of God and expect to see results. According to Hebrews 4:12, "the word of God is quick, powerful, and sharper than any two-edged sword." It is time for us to see some quick and powerful results in our lives, as we defend ourselves using the sword of the spirit.

Before we utter one decree out of our mouths, we must be convinced that we have the power to speak and command the atmosphere to shift. This is why it was important to begin our discussion by reviewing the details of the creation of man. We have established that God simply spoke and whatever He commanded was made manifest. We have also determined that since we were specifically created in the semblance of our Heavenly Father, we have special rights and privileges. These rights afford us the authority to decree a thing and see it established in our lives. We have dominion over the works of God's hands. Therefore, we have the ability to call out into dark places and extract light. We call with the expectation to receive a response. Light must appear!

As you use the declarations in this book to call forth light into dark and stagnant places in your life, have an expectation to experience the creative power of God like never before. Remember you have been created in the image and after the likeness of a God who spoke creation into existence. Now it's time for you to speak peace, prosperity, healing, and restoration with the creative ability handed down to you from your Heavenly Father. It's time to change your world with your words!

HOW TO USE THIS BOOK

1. Select the topic that is most pressing in your life then pray and ask the Holy Spirit to be with you throughout your time of decreeing and declaring God's word. Make sure you do not have any unconfessed sin or unforgiveness in your heart. You don't want anything to negatively impact the effectiveness and power of your declarations.

2. Establish a set time each day for praying and confessing these declarations. A good practice to adopt is confessing your declarations when you get up in the morning, midday and before you retire for the evening. Remember David prayed evening, morning, and noon!

3. Speak each declaration out loud, and ask the Holy Spirit to release revelation concerning that particular area of your life. Believe that God will reveal His will to you as you confess His word.

3. Ask God to show you how to practically apply the spiritual principles that are being decreed and declared to your everyday life!

4. As you speak each declaration, do so with boldness and authority. Again, make sure that you are speaking them out loud, and not just reading them. You may even want to repeat each declaration multiple times until it resonates in your mind and your spirit.

5. Find a time during the day to actually go to each scripture in the Bible and read it in its entirety. Begin journaling each day in order to retain those things that are revealed and any

instruction that you may get during your time of prayer and while you are decreeing and declaring.

6. Make sure you take your declarations with you as you go about your daily routine. Have them readily available to read and repeat throughout your day. The more you repeat the declarations, the more of a reality they will become to you. Take a picture of them with your phone, so you can easily access them. You may also want to use your phone to record yourself as you decree and declare. This way you can listen to yourself repeatedly throughout the day.

7. Be consistent in decreeing and declaring over each of these areas of your life. No matter what you see or don't see happening continue to stand fast on your declaration. Continue to say it until you see it!!

8. Share the declarations with those individuals you encounter throughout the day. Tell someone else about the power of the word of God. Take every opportunity to speak the word over someone else's life!!

Decree, Declare, and Expect God to Move!!

Pastor Kimberly Jones

PURPOSE

Created On Purpose and For Purpose

1. Proverbs 15:22 – I decree I will accomplish my purpose without frustration as I seek and obtain wise counsel!

2. Proverbs 19:21 – I decree that the Lord's plan for my purpose will supersede the plans of man!

3. Ephesians 3:20 – I decree that God will do more than I could every ask or think, as I pursue my purpose and exercise His power that is within me!

4. Exodus 9:16 – As I walk out my purpose, I decree that the power of God is being revealed in my life and I will proclaim His name throughout all of the earth!

5. Isaiah 14:24 – I decree that God's thoughts about me will come to pass and those things He has purposed for my life shall stand!

6. Psalm 57:2 – I decree that my purpose will manifest as God is performing all things on my behalf and completing that which He has begun in me!

7. Ecclesiastes 3:1 – I decree that I will not miss the appointed season and time for my purpose to manifest!

8. Isaiah 46:10 – I decree that God's counsel will stand concerning my purpose and He will do with me as He pleases from the beginning to the end!

9. Psalm 138:8 – I decree that the Lord is perfecting those things concerning my purpose and will not forsake the works of His hands!

10. Romans 8:28 – I decree that as I walk out my purpose all things are working together for my good because I love the Lord and I am called according to His purpose!

NOTES:

_____

_____

_____

_____

_____

_____

_____

_____

_____

_____

_____

_____

_____

_____

_____

_____

_____

_____

_____

_____

_____

_____

_____

_____

_____

WISDOM

Seeking God's Wisdom

1. Proverbs 4:7 – I decree that wisdom is my portion, and with wisdom I also have understanding!

2. Proverbs 9:6 – Today, I will forsake the foolish and live, as I go in the way of understanding!

3. James 1:5-6 – I decree that I will never hesitate to ask God for wisdom when I need it and He will give it to me liberally!

4. Ephesians 5:15-16 – Today, I will walk in wisdom and not foolishness believing that God will redeem the time for me!

5. Proverbs 16:16 – Today, I choose to seek after wisdom and understanding for they are better than silver and gold!

6. Proverbs 13:10 – I decree that I will walk in wisdom today and seek Godly advice!

7. I Corinthians 3:18 – Today, I will seek the wisdom of God and not the wisdom of this world!

8. Proverbs 19:8 – Today, as an act of love to myself, I will get wisdom, seek understanding, and find good!

9. Matthew 7:24 – I decree that I am wise, and I will build my life upon the solid rock of God's word!

10. Isaiah 55:8 – Today, I surrender my thoughts unto the Lord and seek His wisdom, because His thoughts are not my thoughts and His ways are not my ways. His wisdom will guide me today!

NOTES:

_____

_____

_____

_____

_____

_____

_____

_____

_____

_____

_____

AND YOU SHALL DECREE A THING!

_____

_____

_____

_____

_____

_____

_____

_____

_____

_____

_____

_____

PEACE

Peaceful Living

1. Romans 8:6 – Today, I embrace life and peace as I set my mind on the things of the Spirit!

2. John 16:33 – Today, I will have peace, even in the face of tribulation, because God has overcome the world!

3. I Peter 3:10-11 – I decree that I love my life and will see good days as I refrain my tongue and lips from evil and seek peace!

4. John 14:27 – Today, I will not allow my heart to be troubled and I will not be afraid because I have the peace that God has given to me!

5. Colossians 3:15 – I decree that the peace of God is ruling in my heart now and forever!

6. Isaiah 26:3 – Today, I will keep my mind stayed on the Lord and He will keep me in perfect peace because I trust Him!

7. Jude 1:2 – I decree that mercy, love and peace are being multiplied in my life right now!

8. Psalm 119:165 – I decree that I will always have great peace because I love God's law and nothing will make me stumble!

9. Philippians 4:9 – I decree that God's peace will always be with me because I will do those things that I have learned, heard, and seen in Him!

10. Philippians 4:7 – I decree that the peace of God, which surpasses all understanding, will keep my heart and mind today through Christ Jesus!

NOTES:

_____

_____

_____

_____

_____

_____

_____

_____

_____

_____

_____

_____

_____

_____

_____

_____

_____

_____

_____

_____

_____

_____

_____

_____

LOVE

Walking in God's Love

1. Romans 5:8 – I decree that I am loved by God and I will love others unconditionally, because Jesus died for me while I was still a sinner!

2. I John 3:18 – Today, I will not only love in word, but I will love in deed and in truth!

3. Ephesians 4:2-3 – Today, I will be eager to love others and maintain unity of the spirit and the bond of peace!

4. Leviticus 19:18 – Today, I will not hold any grudges and I will love my neighbor as I love myself!

5. Deuteronomy 6:5 – I decree that I love the Lord my God with all my heart, soul, and might!

6. Matthew 5:44 – I will love my enemies, bless them that curse me, do good to them that hate me, and pray for them that use and persecute me!

7. John 15:12 – Today, I will love my family, friends, and neighbors as Jesus has loved me!

8. Romans 8:35 – I decree that NOTHING will separate me from the love of Christ!

9. Ephesians 3: 17 – I decree that Christ dwells in my heart by faith and I will remain rooted and grounded in love!

10. I John 4:12 – I decree that God's love dwells in me and will continue to be perfected in me as I love others!

NOTES:

_____

_____

_____

_____

_____

_____

_____

_____

_____

_____

_____

_____

AND YOU SHALL DECREE A THING!

_____

_____

_____

_____

_____

_____

_____

_____

_____

_____

_____

_____

_____

MARRIAGE

Healthy Holy Matrimony

1. Hebrews 13:4 – I decree that my marriage is honorable, precious, and worth great price and I will hold it in high esteem!

2. Hebrews 10:24 – Today, I will be sure to carefully consider my spouse and will influence him/her into love and good works!

3. Ephesians 5:21 – I decree that my spouse and I are submitting ourselves to each other in the fear of the Lord!

4. I Corinthians 13:7 – I decree that my marriage is strong and founded in love that is able to bear up under anything and everything that comes!

5. Matthew 17:20 – I decree that I have the faith to speak to any mountain that presents itself in my marriage and nothing shall be impossible for me and my spouse!

6. Jeremiah 1:19 – I decree that even though the enemy may fight against my marriage, he will not prevail against it because the Lord is with us to deliver us!

7. Ecclesiastes 4:9 – I decree that my spouse and I will have a good reward for our labor as we work together!

8. Psalm 9:10 – I decree that my marriage is secure because we put our trust in the Lord because we know His name and He will not forsake us!

9. II Corinthians 4:17 – I decree that my marriage is producing God's glory in my life, so I will not complain about light afflictions that may arise!

10. Luke 18:1 – I decree that God is hearing and answering my prayers as they pertain to my marriage. I will not give up and I will not faint!

NOTES:

_____

_____

_____

_____

_____

_____

_____

_____

_____

_____

_____

CHILDREN

Speaking Life Into My Seed

1. Ephesians 6:4 – I decree that my children are being brought up in the nurture and the admonition of the Lord and will always serve Him!

2. Psalm 127:3 – I decree that my children are a heritage of the Lord and a reward unto Him!

3. Exodus 20:6 – I decree that my children are recipients of the blessings and love of the Lord that He has promised to a thousand generations!

4. Proverbs 22:6 – I decree that my children will always walk in the way in which they have been raised and will not depart from the Lord!

5. Ecclesiastes 12:1 – I decree that my children are taking pleasure in God serving Him in the days of their youth!!

6. Isaiah 54:13 – I decree that my children shall be taught of the Lord and great shall be their peace!

7. Isaiah 45:8 – I decree that salvation and righteousness are springing up in my children!

8. Psalm 25:4 – I decree that my children know the ways and the path of the Lord and will follow Him always!

9. II Chronicles 16:9 – I decree that the eyes of the Lord are upon my children and He will show Himself strong and mighty on their behalf!

10. Deuteronomy 28:7 – I decree that every enemy that would rise up against my children will be struck down and put to flight!

NOTES:

_____

_____

_____

_____

_____

_____

_____

_____

_____

_____

_____

_____

AND YOU SHALL DECREE A THING!

_____

_____

_____

_____

_____

_____

_____

_____

_____

_____

_____

_____

_____

MIND

Establishing The Mind of Christ

1. Matthew 22:37 – I decree that I love the Lord with all my heart, and with all my soul, and with all my mind!

2. I Corinthians 2:16 – I decree that I have the mind of Christ!

3. I John 4:4 – I decree that greater is He that is in me and in my mind than he that is in the world!

4. II Timothy 1:7 – I decree that my mind is sound and I will not operate in fear!

5. Colossians 3:1 – I decree that I am in Christ therefore, I will focus and concentrate on the things that are above!

6. Philippians 4:7 – I decree that the peace of God is keeping my heart and my mind in Christ Jesus!

7. II Corinthians 10:4 – I pull down every stronghold that has been built up in my mind with the weapons of the word, prayer, and faith!

8. Philippians 4:8 – I will only think on those things that are true, honest, just, pure, lovely and of a good report!

9. Philippians 4:6 – I will not allow my thoughts to make me anxious, but I will take all of my cares to God in prayer!

10. II Corinthians 10:5 – I cancel every thought in my mind that would exalt itself against the knowledge of God and I bring it into obedience of Christ!

NOTES:

_____

_____

_____

_____

_____

_____

_____

_____

_____

_____

_____

_____

FINANCES

I Have More Than Enough!

1. Genesis 39:23 – I decree that I will always be at a financial advantage because God is causing all that I do to prosper!

2. Ephesians 3:20 – I decree that I have more than enough because I serve a God that is and does more than I could ever ask or thing!

3. Deuteronomy 15:16 – I decree that I am the lender and not the borrower and my finances are overflowing!

4. Psalm 37:25 – I decree that God has not forsaken in the area of my finances and I will never have to beg for bread!

5. Deuteronomy 28:2 – I decree that the blessings of the Lord are coming upon me and financial blessings are overtaking me now because of my obedience!

6. Proverbs 13:22 – I decree that I am righteous and the wealth of the sinner that is laid up for me is being released now!

7. Deuteronomy 8:18 – I decree that I will use the power of my gifts, talents, and anointing to produce wealth in my life!

8. I Peter 2:9 – I decree that I am a royal priesthood and I have been delivered from the darkness of poverty!

9. Proverbs 10:22 – I decree that the blessings of the Lord are making me rich and adding no sorrow with it!

10. Proverbs 13:22 – I decree that I am financially stable and I will leave an inheritance to my children's children!

NOTES:

_____

_____

_____

_____

_____

_____

_____

_____

_____

_____

_____

_____

_____

_____

_____

_____

_____

_____

_____

_____

_____

_____

_____

_____

SUCCESS

You Can Do This!

1. Deuteronomy 28:2 – I decree that success will always find me, come upon me, and overtake me because I am obedient to the Lord!

2. Philippians 4:13 – I decree that God has strengthened me and I can do all things and experience success in every area of my life!

3. Psalm 37:4 – I will delight in the Lord and He will give me the desires of my heart!

4. Psalm 1:3 – I decree that whatever I do will prosper as I consistently take pleasure in the God's word!

5. Proverbs 16:3 – All of my plans for my success in life are committed unto God and He will establish them!

6. I Kings 2:3 – I will prosper in all that I do and everywhere that I go because I am honoring that which God is requiring of me!

7. Luke 16:11 – Great wealth and true riches will be released into my hands because I have been faithful over the little that God has given me!

8. Deuteronomy 8:18 – I decree that I have the power to get wealth because God gave it to me! I will exercise my power NOW!!

9. Jeremiah 17:7 – I am successful in all that I do because I trust the Lord and my hope is in Him!

10. Matthew 6:33 – I will always put God first in my life, and everything that I need to be successful is being added unto me!

NOTES:

_____

_____

_____

_____

_____

_____

_____

_____

_____

_____

_____

_____

CONSISTENCY

When You Find Yourself Wavering

1. Matthew 5:37 – I decree that in all that I do and say, my yes will be yes and my no will be no!

2. I Corinthians 15:58 – I decree that I will be steadfast and unmovable in that which God has called me to do always abounding in the work of the Lord!

3. Luke 16:13 – I decree that I will stand firmly in my faith knowing that I cannot serve two masters!

4. Matthew 6:24 – Today, I will be consistent in my communication letting my yes, be yes and my no, be no!!

5. Galatians 6:9 – I will not get weary in my well doing because in due season I will reap!

6. Titus 2:7 – Today, I will be an example and pattern of good works and good deeds

7. James 1:6 – Today, as I seek the face of the Father, I will do so in faith with nothing wavering!

8. Ecclesiastes 9:10 – I decree that I will carry out my purpose with all my might today and every day!

9. Romans 4:20 – Today, I give God glory, and I will not doubt or stagger at His promises!

10. John 4:34 – Today, I will diligently do the will of Him who sent me and accomplish His work!

NOTES:

_____

_____

_____

_____

_____

_____

_____

_____

_____

_____

_____

_____

_____

_____

_____

_____

_____

_____

_____

_____

_____

_____

_____

_____

PERSEVERANCE

When You Feel Like Giving Up

1. Luke 22:32 – I decree that my faith is strong and it will not fail in difficult times!

2. Romans 12:12 – No matter what I will be patient in tribulation, rejoice in hope, and consistent in prayer!

3. Colossians 1:11 – I decree that I am strengthened with God's glorious power and I will be patient be joyful in difficult times!

4. Galatians 6:9 – I decree my harvest is on the way and I will not get weary or tired in my assignment!

5. James 1:12 – I will persevere under trials knowing that I will receive the victor's crown!

6. II Thessalonians 3:13 – I decree that I will not become weary or disheartened as I do the will of the Father!

7. John 15:7 – I decree that whatever I ask of God will be done for me as I remain in Him and His word remains in me!

8. Ephesians 6:11 – I have on the full armor of God and I will stand and fight against the devices and strategies of the devil!

9. Hebrews 6:11 – I decree that I will consistently display diligence and sincerity and remain hopeful throughout every trial!

10. I Timothy 4:1 – I will not depart from the faith or give myself over to the evil ways of the enemy!

NOTES:

_____

_____

_____

_____

_____

_____

_____

_____

_____

_____

_____

_____

KIMBERLY JONES

JOY

Releasing God's Joy

1. I Peter 1:8 – I decree that I have unspeakable joy because of my love and belief in the Lord!

2. Psalm 30:5 – I decree that joy is my portion, weeping is over, and favour is upon my life!

3. Psalm 5:11 – I decree that my trust is in the Lord and I will shout for joy because He is my defense!

4. Isaiah 55:12 – I decree that as I come and go, I will do so with joy and be lead with peace!

5. Habakkuk 3:18 – Today, I will joy in the God of my salvation and rejoice in Him!

6. John 15:11 – I decree that the joy of the Lord remains in me and it is full!

7. John 16:20 – I decree that all of my sorrow shall be turned into joy!

8. Romans 14:17 – I am a part of the kingdom of God and I have joy and peace in the Holy Ghost!

9. James 1:2 – No matter what I am faced with I will not lose my joy, but I will count it all joy!

10. Nehemiah 8:10 – I decree that the joy of the Lord is my strength!

NOTES:

_____

_____

_____

_____

_____

_____

_____

_____

_____

_____

_____

_____

_____

_____

_____

_____

_____

_____

_____

_____

_____

_____

_____

_____

_____

FEAR

When I Am Afraid

1. Psalm 56:11 – I decree that my trust is in God and I will not operate in fear of man!

2. Genesis 26:24 – I will not fear because God is with me and He will bless me and cause increase in my life!

3. Exodus 14:13 – I am not afraid, but I will stand still and see the salvation of the Lord fight for me and demolish my enemies!

4. II Timothy 1:7 – Today, I will operate in the spirit of power, love, and of a sound mind because God has not given me the spirit of fear!

5. II Kings 6:16 – I decree that there are more for me than against me and I will not fear!

6. Hebrews 13:6 – I decree that the Lord is my helper and I will not fear what man shall do unto me!

7. Psalm 23:4 – I decree that no matter what evil may come upon me I will not fear it because the Lord is with me and He will comfort me!

8. Proverbs 1:33 – I will obey the ways of the Lord and dwell in safety and be quiet from fear!

9. I John 4:18 – I decree that I operate in perfect love and all fear is cast out!

10. Psalm 27:1 – I decree that the Lord is my light, my salvation, and my strength, therefore, I will not fear or be afraid!

NOTES:

_____

_____

_____

_____

_____

_____

_____

_____

_____

_____

_____

_____

FRIENDS

Seeking Godly Friends

1. John 15:13 – I decree that I have friends who love me and will lay down their lives for me and I will do the same for them!

2. Psalm 1:1 – I decree that I will not walk in the counsel of the ungodly, stand in the way of sinners, nor sit in the seat of the scornful!

3. Proverbs 18:24 – Today, I will show myself friendly and God will direct my steps to my God-ordained friends!

4. Job 42:10 – As I pray for my friends today, I decree that God will turn my captivity!

5. I Corinthians 15:33 – I decree that I will only befriend those who will build up my character and not corrupt it!

6. Job 2:11 – I decree that my relationships are mutually beneficial and emotionally supportive!

7. Luke 6:31 – I decree that I will treat my God-ordained friends as I desire to be treated!

8. Proverbs 22:24 – I will not make friends with those who are ill-tempered or easily angered!

9. Proverbs 27:17 – I decree that my friends sharpen me and I sharpen them and we are better together!

10. II Kings 2:2 - I decree that God is bringing friends in my life who I can follow, and who can follow me as we follow Christ!

NOTES:

_____

_____

_____

_____

_____

_____

_____

_____

_____

_____

_____

_____

_____

_____

_____

_____

_____

_____

_____

_____

_____

_____

_____

_____

WORSHIP

Decreeing God's Worth

1. II Samuel 22:4 – I will call on the Lord and worship and praise His name and He will save me from my enemies!

2. Exodus 34:14 – I decree that I will worship no other God besides Jehovah who is worthy to be praised!

3. Philippians 3:3 – I will worship God in spirit, rejoice in Jesus Christ, and have no confidence in my flesh!

4. Psalm 29:2 – Today, I will give unto the Lord the glory He is due and worship Him in the beauty of holiness!

5. John 4:23 – I decree that I will always worship the Father in spirit and in truth!

6. John 9:31- I decree that I am a worshipper of God and I do His will, therefore He will hear me when I cry unto Him!

7. Psalm 31:2 – I decree that as I worship the Lord He will hear me and deliver me speedily and save me!

8. Hebrews 12:28 – I decree that my worship is acceptable unto God as I approach Him with reverence and godly fear!

9. Psalm 95:6 – I decree that the Lord is my maker and I will bow down and worship Him regardless of my situation!

10. Psalm 34:18 – I decree that the Lord is nigh unto me as I worship Him with brokenness of heart and a contrite spirit!

NOTES:

_____

_____

_____

_____

_____

_____

_____

_____

_____

_____

_____

_____

HEALTH

Speaking Strength to My Body

1. Psalm 107:20 – I decree that the word of God is healing me and delivering me from destruction!

2. I Corinthians 6:19 – I decree that my body is the temple of the Holy Ghost and sickness and disease are far from me!

3. III John 1:2 – I decree that I am in good health and prospering in my mind, will, and emotions!

4. Psalm 41:3 – I decree that the Lord is preserving and keeping me alive and healing me when I am sick!

5. Jeremiah 33:6 – I decree that God is bringing healing to my body and is releasing and abundance of peace and truth into my life!

6. Proverbs 3:7-8 – I will not be wise in my own eyes, but fear the lord and depart from evil, and health is my portion!

7. Psalm 30:2 – I decree that as I cry unto the Lord, He will hear me and heal me!

8. Exodus 23:25 – I will serve the Lord my God and He will bless my bread and my water, and take sickness from the midst of me!

9. Isaiah 53:5 – I decree that with the stripes of Jesus I am healed and made whole!

10. Psalm 103:2-3 – I decree that all my diseases are healed by the Father, and I will bless Him!

NOTES:

_____

_____

_____

_____

_____

_____

_____

_____

_____

_____

_____

_____

_____

HOME

Covering My Home With The Word

1. Joshua 24:15 – I decree that I and my house will serve the Lord!

2. Acts 16:31 – I decree that my entire household shall be saved because I believe on the name of the Lord!

3. Psalm 147:14 – I decree that peace shall be in the borders of my home and God will always give us His best!

4. Psalm 133:1-4 – I decree that my household is operating in unity and God is releasing His commanded blessing upon us!

5. I Corinthians 14:40 – I decree that peace and order will manifest in my home at all times!

6. Habakkuk 2:3 – I decree that the vision for my home will come to pass at its appointed time and there will be no delay!

7. II Corinthians 12:9 – I decree that God's grace in fully operating in my home and it is sufficient unto my entire household!

8. Proverbs 9:1 – I decree that my home is established in the wisdom of God!

9. Mark 3:25 – I decree that my house will not be divided against itself and we shall stand!

10. Romans 4:21 – I am fully persuaded that which God has ordained for my household, He will perform as He has promised!

NOTES:

_____

_____

_____

_____

_____

_____

_____

_____

_____

_____

_____

_____

KIMBERLY JONES

SAFETY

When You Feel Unprotected

1. Psalm 17:8 – I decree that I am the apple of God's eye and He will protect and hide me under the shadow of His wings!

2. Deuteronomy 31:6 – I will be strong and courageous because the Lord is with me and will not fail or forsake me!

3. Psalm 91:11 – I decree that angels are watching over me and keeping me in all my ways!

4. Jeremiah 1:19 – I decree that even though the enemy may fight against me, He will not prevail because the Lord is with me to deliver me!

5. Psalm 4:8 – I decree that I am dwelling in the safety and trust of the Lord who allows me to lay down in peace and sleep!

6. John 14:27 – I decree I have the peace of God and I will not allow my heart to be troubled and I will not be afraid!

7. John 16:33 – Today, I will be at peace and of good cheer in tribulation because God has already overcome the world!

8. II Thessalonians 3:3 – I decree that the Lord is faithful and He is establishing me and keeping me from evil!

9. Proverbs 18:10 – I decree that the name of the Lord is a strong tower and I run into it and find safety!

10. Psalm 31:20 – I decree that I am hidden in the secret of the presence of the Lord and He is keeping me from the pride of man and tongues of strife!

NOTES:

_____

_____

_____

_____

_____

_____

_____

_____

_____

_____

AND YOU SHALL DECREE A THING!

COURAGE

When You Must Stand

1. I Chronicles 19:13 – I decree that I will always behave myself valiantly with courage knowing that the Lord will do that which is good in His sight!

2. Joshua 1:9 – I will be strong and of good courage and I will not be dismayed or afraid for the Lord is with me wherever I go!

3. Psalm 27:14 – Today, I will wait on the Lord and be of good courage and He will strengthen my heart!

4. Judges 20:22 – I decree that I am strong and I will encourage myself and continue to fight and be strong!

5. Ephesians 6:11 – Today, I will be strong in the Lord and the power of His might!

6. Psalm 118:6 – I decree that the Lord is on my side and I will not fear what man can do to me!

7. II Timothy 1:7 – I decree that I have the power, love, and sound mind that God has given to me and I will not be afraid!

8. Psalm 46:1 – I decree that God is my refuge, my strength, and a very present help in trouble!

9. Joel 3:10 – I decree that I am strong no matter how weak I feel and I will overcome the enemy!

10. Romans 8:31 – I decree that God is for me, therefore nothing and no one can be against me or overcome me!

NOTES:

_____

_____

_____

_____

_____

_____

_____

_____

_____

_____

_____

_____

DIFFICULT TIMES

When Trouble Finds You

1. II Samuel 22:18 – I decree that when my enemy is too strong for me, the Lord will deliver me!

2. Isaiah 59:19 – I decree that when the enemy comes in like a flood the Spirit of the Lord will always raise a standard against him!

3. Nahum 1:7 – I decree that the Lord is a stronghold in the day of trouble and I will trust Him!

4. Psalm 30:5 – I decree that my weeping will not endure forever but my joy is coming!

5. Psalm 46:1 – I decree that God is my refuge and my strength and a very present help in trouble!

6. Psalm 33:2 – I decree that I will wait on God and He will be my strength and salvation in the time of trouble!

7. Isaiah 55:6 – In my times of trouble I will seek the Lord, find Him, and call on Him while He is near!

8. Acts 16:25 – I decree that I will be delivered from trouble when I pray and sing praises unto God!

9. Ephesians 3:20 – I decree that God will do exceedingly and abundantly above all I ask or think according to the power working in me!

10. James 1:12 – I decree that I am blessed, even in the midst of trouble, knowing I will receive that which has been promised to me!

NOTES:

_____

_____

_____

_____

_____

_____

_____

_____

_____

_____

_____

AND YOU SHALL DECREE A THING!

_____

_____

_____

_____

_____

_____

_____

_____

_____

_____

_____

_____

_____

HUSBAND

Mighty Man of Valor

1. Ephesians 5:25 – I decree that my husband loves me as Christ loves the church and give of himself freely!

2. Judges 6:12 – I decree that my husband is a mighty man of valor and God is with him!

3. Psalm 128:2 – I decree that my husband shall eat and provide according to the labor of his hands; he shall be happy, and it shall be well with him!

4. I Peter 3:7 – I decree that my husband is honoring me and dwelling with me according to knowledge and we are heirs together of the grace of life!

5. Romans 8:14 – I decree that my husband is a son of God because He is led by the Spirit!

6. Luke 18:1 – I decree that my husband is a man of prayer and he will not faint, lose heart, or give up!

7. II Corinthians 5:17 – I decree that God has made all things new in my husband's life and old things are passed away!

8. Ephesians 1:11 – I decree that God is working at all things concerning my husband after the counsel of His own will!

9. Psalm 1:1 – I decree that my husband is blessed because he is not walking in the counsel of the ungodly, standing in the way of sinners, nor sitting in the seat of the scornful!

10. Numbers 14:8 – I decree that God delights in my husband and is bringing him into his season of manifested promises!

NOTES:

_____

_____

_____

_____

_____

_____

_____

_____

_____

_____

_____

WIFE

The Virtuous Woman

1. Psalms 143:8 – I decree that my wife will always hear thy lovingkindness in the morning and you will lead her and lift her soul unto you!

2. Proverbs 31:25 – I decree that my wife is clothed with strength and honor!

3. Proverbs 14:1 – I decree that my wife is wise and she is building her house up and not tearing it down!

4. Jeremiah 29:13 – I decree that my wife is seeking God with her whole heart and finding Him in her time of need!

5. Galatians 5:22 – I decree that the fruit of the Spirit is always evident in my wife's life as she shows love, joy, peace, longsuffering, gentleness, goodness, faith, meekness, and temperance!

6. Luke 1:45 – I decree that there shall be a performance of the promises spoken by the Lord about my wife's life!

7. Proverbs 31:12 – I decree that my wife will strengthen, comfort, and encourage her family and always do good by them.

8. Psalm 28:7 – I decree that my wife will find strength and protection in the Lord and her heart will trust in Him!

9. Philippians 4:7 – I decree that the peace of God is my wife's portion and it is keeping her heart and mind in Christ Jesus!

10. III John 1:3 – I decree that my wife is prospering and abiding in health in her body, mind, and soul!

NOTES:

_____

_____

_____

_____

_____

_____

_____

_____

_____

_____

_____

AND YOU SHALL DECREE A THING!

_____

_____

_____

_____

_____

_____

_____

_____

_____

_____

_____

_____

_____

FAVOR

Favor Will Find Me

1. Psalm 118:24 – This is the day which the Lord hath made, I will rejoice and be glad in it!

2. James 4:10 – Today, I will humble myself in the sight of the Lord, knowing that He will lift me up and show me favor!

3. Psalms 138:8 – I decree that the Lord is perfecting that which concerns me and He will never forsake me!

4. Psalm 41:11 – I decree that God's favor is on my life and the enemy will not triumph over me!

5. I Samuel 2:26 – I decree that I have the favor of God and the favor of man upon my life!

6. Psalm 35:27 – I decree that the Lord favors my cause and takes pleasure in my prosperity!

7. Proverbs 13:15 - I decree that good understanding will always be my portion and will cause me to obtain favor!

8. Proverbs 21:1 – I decree that the heart of the kings is in the Lord's hand and He will turn it for my favor!

9. Romans 8:31 – I decree that God is for me and nothing and no one can be against me!

10. Psalm 118:6 – I decree that the Lord is on my side and I have favor with Him and man can do NOTHING to me!

NOTES:

_____

_____

_____

_____

_____

_____

_____

_____

_____

_____

_____

KIMBERLY JONES

BUSINESS

Blessings Over My Business

1. Psalm 118:24 – This is the day which the Lord hath made, I will rejoice and be glad in it!

2. Jeremiah 29:11 – I decree that God is thinking thoughts of peace about me and my business and my expected end is full of success!

3. I Thessalonians 5:16-18 – I will always rejoice over my business no matter what the circumstances for this is God's will for me!

4. Proverbs 12:1 – I decree that I will always be open to instruction and knowledge when it comes to conducting business matters!

5. Hebrews 6:7 – I decree that I will always operate my business with good will by serving others in a way that is pleasing to God!

6. Isaiah 40:31 – I decree that I will wait patiently on the Lord concerning my business matters and He will give me strength!

7. Romans 8:28 – I decree that all things concerning my business are working together for my good because I love God and have been called for purpose!

8. Psalm 37:4 – I will delight myself in the Lord and He will give me the desires of my heart for my business!

9. Matthew 7:7 – I decree that every door that I knock on for the growth of my business will be opened unto me!

10. James 2:6 – I decree that I will exercise my faith by working diligently in my business knowing that faith without works is dead!

NOTES:

_____

_____

_____

_____

_____

_____

_____

_____

_____

_____

_____

_____

AND YOU SHALL DECREE A THING!

EMOTIONS

STABILIZING MY EMOTIONS

1. Proverbs 16:32 – I decree that I am mighty because I am always slow to anger!

2. Philippians 4:7 – I decree that the peace of God which surpasses all understanding is keeping my heart and mind through Christ Jesus!

3. Colossians 3:2 – I decree that I am emotionally stable because my mind is set on things above and not on things of the earth!

4. Psalm 139:23-24 – I decree that any wicked emotion cannot remain as God searches, tries, and knows my thoughts!

5. Philippians 4:6 – I decree that I will let my requests be made known unto God and I will not fret or be anxious about anything!

6. II Timothy 1:7 – I decree that I do not operate in the spirit of fear, but in power, love, and soundness of mind!

7. Nehemiah 8:10 – I decree that I have the joy of the Lord and sadness is far from me!

8. Isaiah 61:3 – I decree that the spirit of heaviness will not have rule over me and I am covered with the garment of praise!

9. Proverbs 17:22 – I decree that I have a merry heart and I am emotionally healed!

10. II Timothy 1:7 – I decree that my emotions are stable and I will not operate in fear but power, love, and soundness of mind!

NOTES:

_____

_____

_____

_____

_____

_____

_____

_____

_____

_____

_____

_____

_____

_____

_____

_____

_____

_____

_____

_____

_____

_____

_____

_____

NATION

PRAYING FOR THE NATION

1. I Timothy 2:1-2 – I decree that my prayers for those in authority in this nation will produce peace and quiet in all godliness and holiness!

2. Romans 13:1 – I decree that all authority has been established by God in this nation!

3. Jeremiah 29:7 – I decree the Lord's peace and prosperity over this nation, when the nation prospers so will I!

4. II Chronicles 7:14 – I decree that God is hearing from heaven as we pray, forgiving the sins of this nation and healing our land!

5. Psalms 2:10-11 – I decree that the rulers of this nation will serve the Lord with fear and celebrate His rule!

6. Proverbs 11:14 – I decree Godly guidance over this nation and victory will be won for this country through many wise counselors!

7. Proverbs 21:1 – I decree that the hearts of this nation's rulers is as a stream of water in the hands of the Lord!

8. Joel 3:12 – I decree that this nation will be awakened out of spiritual stupor and serve God!

9. Haggai 2:7 – I decree that this nation is being shaken and the desires of this nation will come to the Lord!

10. Galatians 3:8 – I decree that this nation is blessed through God's people!

NOTES:

_____

_____

_____

_____

_____

_____

_____

_____

_____

_____

_____

_____

_____

_____

_____

_____

_____

_____

_____

_____

_____

_____

_____

_____

_____

FORGIVENESS

Forgiving and Forgiven

1. Ephesians 4:32 – I decree that am kind, tenderhearted, and forgiving to others, as God has forgiven me!

2. James 5:16 – I confess my faults and pray for others that I might be healed and forgiven of my sins!

3. Luke 6:37 – I decree that I will not judge or condemn those who have hurt, rejected, or offended me!

4. Psalm 51:10 – I decree that God is creating a clean heart in me void of all bitterness and unforgiveness!

5. Matthew 7:12 – I will extend the forgiveness, love and mercy to others as I desire others to do the same for me!

6. Psalm 103:12 – I decree that I have been forgiven of all my transgressions and they are as far from me as the east is from the west!

7. Psalm 130:4 – I decree that there is forgiveness with the Lord and He is to be reverently feared and worshipped!

8. Isaiah 43:25 – I decree that my transgressions have been blotted out for my sake and my sins are remembered no more!

9. Colossians 3:13 – I decree that I will be gentle and forbear with others and will pardon others as God has pardoned me!

10. I Peter 4:8 – I decree that I have intense and unfailing love for others and I will disregard and forgive the offenses of others!

NOTES:

_____

_____

_____

_____

_____

_____

_____

_____

_____

_____

_____

BLESSINGS

Releasing Blessings Over My Life

1. Exodus 23:25 – I decree that I will serve the Lord and He will bless my bread and my water and sickness will be taken from the midst of me!

2. Proverbs 10:22 – I decree the blessings of the Lord are making me rich and adding no sorrow with it!

3. Deuteronomy 28:2 – I decree that all of the blessings of God will come upon me and overtake me as I walk in obedience to God's word!

4. Deuteronomy 7:9 – I decree that the covenant blessings of God are upon my life and will last to a thousand generations with those who love Him!

5. Luke 1:28 – I decree that I am highly favored, God is with me and I am blessed among many!

6. Psalm 133:3 – I decree the commanded blessing of the Lord over my life and over my family!

7. Proverbs 28:20 – I decree that I am faithful and blessings are abounding in my life!

8. Psalm 40:4 – I decree that I am blessed because I make the Lord my trust and I turn away from lies!

9. Ephesians 1:3 – I decree that I am blessed with all spiritual blessings in heavenly places!

10. James 1:17 – I decree that I am blessed with every perfect gift from above that comes down from the Father!

NOTES:

_____

_____

_____

_____

_____

_____

_____

_____

_____

_____

_____

_____

_____

_____

_____

_____

_____

_____

_____

_____

_____

_____

_____

_____

ATTITUDE

When I Need An Attitude Adjustment

1. Mark 9:50 – I decree that I am the salt of the earth and I will not lose my savour through a bad attitude or evil disposition!

2. Proverbs 17:22 – I decree that my heart is merry and cheerful and my spirit is alive!

3. Psalm 16:11 – I decree that I have the fullness of joy, as I remain in the presence of the Lord!

4. Colossians 4:6 – I decree that my speech will always be seasoned with grace and I will respond to others properly!

5. Philippians 4:4 – I decree that I will always rejoice in the Lord even when I am not at my best!

6. Romans 12:14-15 – I decree that I will bless them that persecute me and rejoice with them that rejoice!

7. Isaiah 26:3 – I decree that I am in perfect peace because my mind is stayed upon the Lord!

8. Proverbs 16:24 – I will speak pleasant words that are sweet to the soul and health to the bones!

9. Galatians 5:22-23 – I decree that my life and my attitude will always reflect the fruit of the Spirit which is love, joy, peace, patience, kindness, goodness, faithfulness, gentleness, and self-control!

10. Psalm 118:24 – I decree that this is the day that the Lord has made and I will rejoice and be glad in it!

NOTES:

_____

_____

_____

_____

_____

_____

_____

_____

_____

_____

_____

_____

DOUBLE-MINDEDNESS

When I Am Torn In My Mind

1. James 1:8 – I decree that I am stable in all my ways and double mindedness is far from me!

2. James 4:8 – I decree that my heart is purified, my hands are clean and when I draw near to God, He will draw near to me!

3. Isaiah 29:13 – I decree that I am near to God and honor Him with my mouth and my heart and my fear for Him is genuine!

4. I Kings 18:21 – I decree that the Lord is God and I will follow Him and never hesitate between two opinions!

5. Matthew 6:24 – I decree settled in my faith and I will not serve two masters; I love the Lord and Him only!

6. Matthew 5:37 – I decree that my yes will be yes and my no will be no and evil is not my portion!

7. Luke 10:27 – I decree that I love the Lord my God with all my heart, soul, strength, and mind!

8. Deuteronomy 30:19 – Today, I choose life and not death that me and my seed may live!

9. Isaiah 26:3 – I decree that my mind is in perfect peace because it is stayed on the Lord and I trust in Him!

10. Psalm 4:2I decree that I am delivered from the pit of destruction of doublemindedness and I am established in my goings!

NOTES:

_____

_____

_____

_____

_____

_____

_____

_____

_____

_____

_____

_____

_____

_____

_____

_____

_____

_____

_____

_____

_____

_____

_____

_____

_____

CONFIDENCE

When My Confidence Is Wavering

1. Hebrews 10:35 – I decree that I will hold onto my confidence because there is great reward in doing so!

2. Psalm 27:3 – I decree that I will be confident and not fear in the midst of opposition and distress!

3. Philippians 1:6 – I am confident that God will complete the good work that He has begun in me!

4. II Corinthians 10:7 – I decree that I belong to Christ and my confidence in this will not be shaken!

5. Galatians 5:10 – I decree that I am stable-minded and my confidence will not be taken by my enemies!

6. Psalm 27:13 – I decree that I will not faint because I am confident that I will see the goodness of the Lord in the land of the living!

7. Luke 18:9 – I decree that my confidence is not in myself but in God!

8. I John 2:28 – I decree that I will live, abide, and remain confident in Jesus!

9. Proverbs 3:26 – I decree that the Lord is my confidence and He will keep my feet from slipping into the traps of the enemy!

10. II Corinthians 3:5 – I decree that I am confident because my sufficiency is in God and not in myself!

NOTES:

_____

_____

_____

_____

_____

_____

_____

_____

_____

_____

_____

BOLDNESS

When I Feel Weak

1. Ephesians 3:12 – I decree that I have boldness and access to God by faith in Jesus Christ!

2. Proverbs 28:1 – I decree that I am righteous and bold as a lion!

3. Acts 4:13 - I decree that my life in Jesus is making bold to do great works for the kingdom!

4. Acts 4:29 – I decree that I will not be intimidated by the enemy and will always speak the word with boldness!

5. Hebrews 13:6 – I decree that the Lord is my helper and I will not fear what man shall do unto me and I will not be stopped!

6. Philippians 1:20 – I decree that Christ will boldly be manifested in my life as I live to bring God glory!

7. Hebrews 4:16 – I decree that I am bold in approaching God in prayer and will approach the throne of grace in expectation and anticipation!

8. II Corinthians 10:2 – I decree that I will walk in the spirit and not in my flesh and be bold in the Lord!

9. Jeremiah 1:8 – I decree that I will not be afraid of the faces of men because God is with me to deliver me!

10. Romans 8:31 – I decree that I am unafraid and can do all things because God is for me!

NOTES:

_____

_____

_____

_____

_____

_____

_____

_____

_____

_____

_____

_____

_____

_____

_____

_____

_____

_____

_____

_____

_____

_____

_____

DEPRESSION

When I Need Joy

1. Nehemiah 8:10 – I decree that the joy of the Lord is my strength!

2. Isaiah 61:3 – I decree that I am covered with a garment of praise and the spirit of heaviness has to go now!

3. Psalm 30:11 – I decree that my mourning is turned into dancing and I am girded with gladness!

4. Psalm 30:5 – I decree that it's a new day, my weeping is over and joy is mine!

5. I Thessalonians 5:18 – I decree that no matter what is going on in my life I will give God thanks!

6. Psalm 118:24 – I decree that this is the day that the Lord has made and I will rejoice and be glad in it!

7. Isaiah 59:19 – I decree that a standard is being raised by the Spirit of the Lord over every attack against my mind and my thoughts!

8. II Corinthians 10:5 – I decree that every evil imagination the enemy would try to create in my mind is cast down right now!

9. II Corinthians 10:5 – I decree that my thoughts are taken captive to the obedience of Christ!

10. Psalm 142:7 – I decree that my soul is brought out of the prison of depression and I will praise the name of the Lord!

NOTES:

_____

_____

_____

_____

_____

_____

_____

_____

_____

_____

_____

_____

_____

_____

_____

_____

_____

_____

_____

_____

_____

_____

_____

_____

DETERMINATION

I CAN'T GIVE UP

1. Psalm 119:133 – I decree that my steps are ordered in the word of God and iniquity will not have rule over me!

2. Proverbs 11:1 – I decree that I am balanced and my life is bringing glory to God!

3. James 1:6 – I decree that by faith I will be consistent in my walk and not waver and receive all that God has promised for my life!

4. Matthew 5:37 – I decree that in my communication that my yes will be yes and my no will be no and I will not give up!

5. Matthew 6:24 – I decree that I am serving God and God only because I cannot serve two masters!

6. James 1:8 – I decree that I am single-minded and stable in all of my ways!

7. Luke 9:62 – I decree that my hand is on the plough, I am moving forward and will not look back! I am fit for the kingdom!

8. Hebrews 12:1 – I decree that every weight and sin that pulls me off track is broken off my life and I will run the race before me with faith and patience!

9. Hebrews 13:8 – I decree that I am stable in word and deed because I serve a stable God who is the same yesterday, today, and forever!

10. Ephesians 4:14 – I decree that I will no longer be tossed to and fro and carried about with every wind of doctrine. I know who I am and I know who God is!

NOTES:

_____

_____

_____

_____

_____

_____

_____

_____

_____

_____

_____

_____

STRENGTH

WHEN YOU FEEL POWERLESS

1. Isaiah 41:10 – I decree that the Lord is with me and He will strengthen, help, and uphold me!

2. Philippians 4:13 – I decree that I can do all things through Christ who gives me strength!

3. Psalm 29:11 – I decree that the Lord is giving me strength and blessing me with peace!

4. II Corinthians 12:9 – I decree that God's grace is enough for me and His strength is perfected in weakness!

5. Exodus 15:2 – I decree that the Lord is my strength, my song, and my salvation!

6. Isaiah 40:29 – I decree that when I am weary, the Lord will increase my power and make me strong!

7. Psalm 46:1 – I decree that God is my refuge and my strength and a present help in the time of trouble!

8. Deuteronomy 31:6 – I decree that I am strong and courageous and I will not fear because the Lord is with me!

9. Isaiah 40:31 – I decree that as I wait upon the Lord, He is renewing my strength!

10. Psalm 31:24 – I decree that my hope is in the Lord and He will give me strength and courage!

NOTES:

_____

_____

_____

_____

_____

_____

_____

_____

_____

_____

_____

PROVISION

WHEN I AM IN NEED

1. Philippians 4:19 – I decree that my God will supply all of my needs according to His riches in glory!

2. II Corinthians 9:8 – I decree that God is making all grace abound unto me and I have everything I need!

3. Psalm 111:5 – I decree that God is a covenant keeper and He will provide for me as I fear Him!

4. Psalm 23:1 – I decree that the Lord is my shepherd and I shall not want!

5. Psalm 84:11 – I decree that God is my sun and my shield and He will not withhold any good thing from me!

6. Exodus 23:25 – I decree that the Lord is blessing my bread and my water because I serve Him!

7. II Corinthians 9:10 – I decree that God will continue to provide seeds for me to sow and food for bread!

8. Proverbs 3:10 – I decree that my barns are filled with plenty, and my presses are bursting out with new wine!

9. Psalm 34:10 – I decree that I shall not want any good thing as I seek the Lord!

10. Ephesians 3:20 – I decree that God is doing exceedingly and abundantly above all I ask or think!

NOTES:

_____

_____

_____

_____

_____

_____

_____

_____

_____

_____

_____

_____

CONCLUSION

Job 22:28 – Thou shall also decree a thing, and it shall be established unto thee: and the light shall shine upon thy ways.

In this book, I pray you have discovered that for every situation in your life, there are solutions and answers embedded in God's word. I hope that as you have decreed and declared these scriptures over your life, the light of God's word has illuminated dark places. God is a God of His word. Numbers 23:19 clearly states that He does not lie. If He said it, He will surely bring it to pass.

We must be careful not to equate God's ability to deliver on His promises, with man's ability. In my life, I have experienced the disappointment of unfulfilled promises. Not just one time, but many times over. It never feels good to have your hopes dashed when you have been promised something that never materializes. Nobody wants to be let down. I am grateful that we serve a God who NEVER lets us down.

If we have an expectation for God to come through on His promises to us, we must know what they are. The only way for us to embrace His promises is by having a proper command of the word of God. It's our responsibility to know what the Word says about every area of our lives. God has given us promises that pertain to our families, finances, ministries, and businesses. It is our job to search the scriptures to discover what they are. Once we discover His promises, we must then begin to speak them over our lives every day.......out loud!

In Job 22:28 the word instructs us that if we decree a thing, it shall be established unto us. I like the way the Amplified version expresses this scripture..."You shall **decide** and **decree** a thing, and it shall be established for you, and the light of God's favor shall shine upon your ways." All we have to do is decide in our hearts and minds that God's word is true and then decree it and watch God's favor overtake our lives. Once God shines His favor upon our situation, those things that attempt to evade us, must now stand still under the authority of God's word. We have victory through His promises!

Deciding does not mean that God is following our lead. Deciding is not to say that we create the rules. Deciding means that we come into alignment with what God has already established about our lives. God knew us before we were formed in our mother's womb. Everything about our lives was finalized before we were even born. He thinks good thoughts about us. Now, all we have to do is think good thoughts about ourselves. It all comes down to a simple decision. We must decide that our families are blessed and then begin to decree over them. We must decide that we are whole in our minds, and then decree the word of God over our minds. We must decide that we are living in abundance and then decree what the Word of God says about it and wait and watch for the manifestation. His light will begin to shine upon all of our ways.

When we consistently apply the truths found in the scriptures to situations we are faced with, change is inevitable. God's word is transformational and transitional. It changes our thinking and behaviors. Once we think and behave differently, we find ourselves in new places spiritually, emotionally, mentally, and even financially. As we decree God's word, we are advanced from faith to faith and from glory to glory. The more we ingest the Word, the farther we are advanced in our understanding of who God is and who we are. We begin to know Him in a more intimate way and experience levels of His glory that are only accessible to those who diligently seek Him.

Standing on God's word is not always easy, but it's necessary if we desire to live the abundant life promised in the Word. When we change our words, we change our world. It's time out for you remaining in the same stuck place, waiting for God to rescue you. He has already given you everything that you need to move forward. The power of life and death are in your tongue. All you have to do is open your mouth and boldly confess God's word.

God will meet you at the point of your expectation. If you believe that God is a healer, find out what the Word says about healing and expect God to show up and heal your body. You might need God to transform your mind and pull you up out of depression. He can do just that. He is just waiting for you to believe it, confess it, and trust Him to bring it to pass. The Word of God never changes. It is the same and will continue to be quick, sharp, and powerful until Jesus' return. All we have to do is exercise our faith by putting His words into action. Once we have decreed and declared over a particular area of our lives, it is then time for us to live it.

I have covered quite a few topics in this book, but there are so many more that could have been included. Ask the Holy Spirit to speak to you and show you what you need to pray for and what scriptures you should declare. He will do just that. Just like God inspires me, He will do the same for you.

All the declarations in this book were written through divine revelation of the Holy Spirit. I believe that as you continue to decree and declare over these areas of your life, you are going to begin to experience a shift. Your life is going to be made better. Don't stop decreeing and declaring. Say it until you see it and allow the Word of God to resurrect dead places and create new life for you!

ABOUT THE AUTHOR

 Pastor Kimberly Jones is a "people lover" at heart, and it shows up in every aspect of her life. She is a co-pastor at Prevailing Love Worship Center in Stone Mountain, GA, and owner of Living On Purpose Life & Empowerment Coaching, LLC. In addition to being a Certified Master Life Coach, Kimberly is also a motivational speaker and spiritual mentor/mother to many. She uses her gifts and talents to encourage women and men to maximize their potential by taking ownership of their lives through spiritual awareness and personal development. Her speaking platforms include women's conferences, coaching seminars, and business workshops. She also works with individuals and groups as a Life Coach, compelling them to "Live on Purpose and Make Every Day Count."

Contact Kimberly online at www.kimberlyj.net or via email at livenow@kimberlyj.net.

Made in the USA
Columbia, SC
08 June 2024

36321255R00074